CONVERTING FRACTIONS TO DECIMALS

VOLUME I

Math 5th Grade
Children's Fraction Books

Hi there! What's up?

Let's Discuss about conversion of
fractions to decimals.

Are you Ready?
Okay, let's start!

CONVERTING FRACTIONS TO DECIMAL FORM

A fraction sign $-$ and the division sign $\div$ are the same. So, whenever you see an equation like this, $\frac{1}{2}$.

It means: $\frac{1}{2}$ or $1 \div 2$

How to convert a fraction to decimal

➲ Divide the numerator by the denominator

$\frac{1}{2}$ ← Numerator
     ← Denominator

$$\frac{1}{2} = 1 \div 2 = \boxed{0.5}$$

CONVERTING DECIMALS TO FRACTION FORM

How to convert a decimal to a fraction.

➲ Write down the decimal divided by 1, like this:

$$\frac{0.5}{1}$$

➲ Multiply both top and bottom by 10 for every number after the decimal point. If there are two digits after the decimal point, then use 100, if there are three then use 1000 and so on.

$$\frac{0.5}{1} \quad \frac{\times \ 10}{\times \ 10} = \frac{50}{100}$$

➲ Reduce to lowest term.

$$\frac{50}{100} = \frac{25}{50} = \frac{1}{2}$$

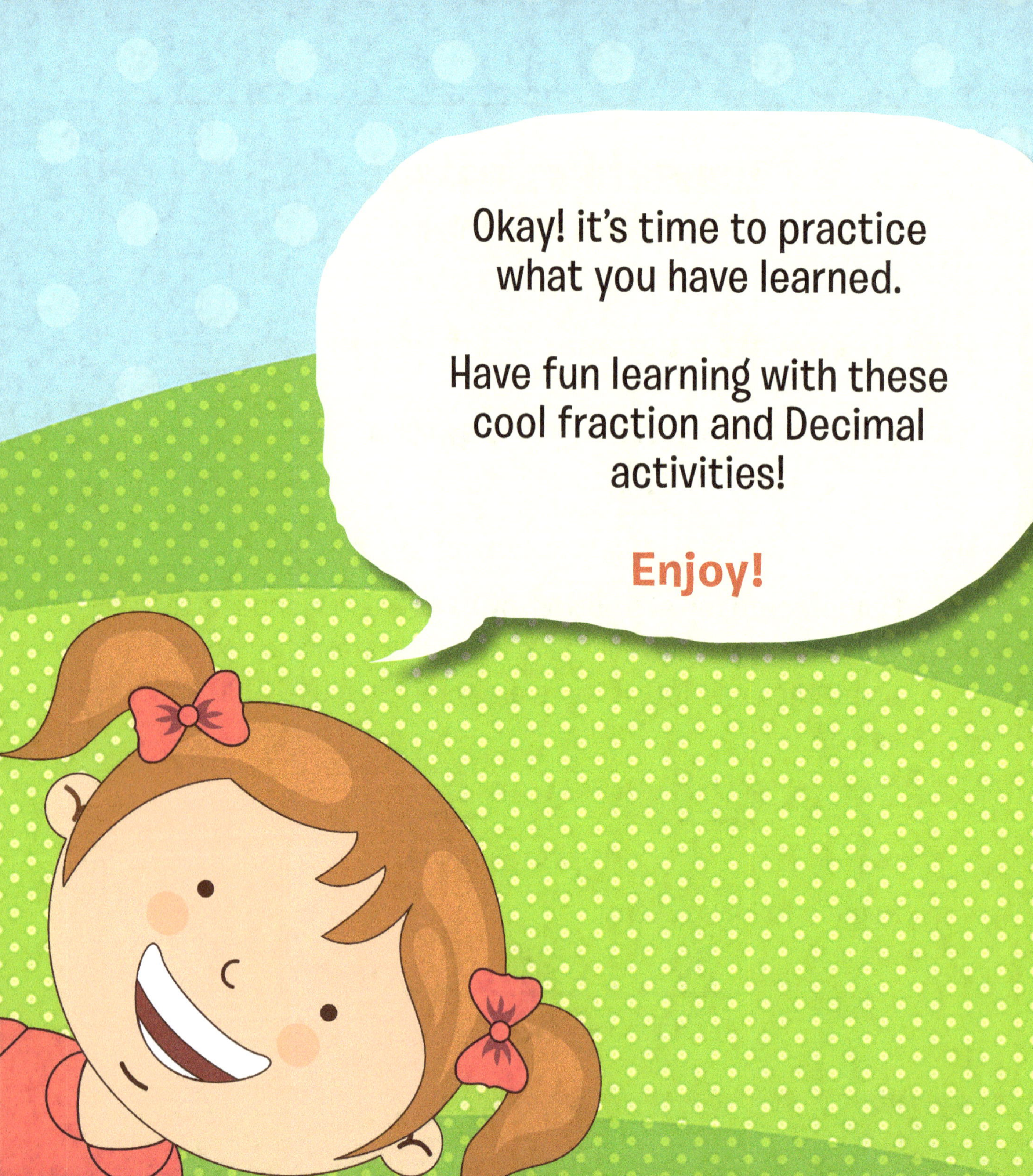

Okay! it's time to practice what you have learned.

Have fun learning with these cool fraction and Decimal activities!

Enjoy!

FRACTIONS TO DECIMALS

Convert the fractions to decimals.

Convert the fractions to decimals.

1) $\dfrac{1}{12}$ =

2) $\dfrac{3}{6}$ =

3) $\dfrac{1}{4}$ =

4) $\dfrac{6}{8}$ =

5) $\dfrac{2}{5}$ =

6) $\dfrac{1}{3}$ =

7) $\dfrac{2}{3}$ =

8) $\dfrac{6}{12}$ =

9) $\dfrac{4}{20}$ =

10) $\dfrac{2}{4}$ =

Convert the fractions to decimals.

1) $\dfrac{5}{10}$ =

2) $\dfrac{2}{8}$ =

3) $\dfrac{5}{6}$ =

4) $\dfrac{1}{8}$ =

5) $\dfrac{6}{10}$ =

6) $\dfrac{7}{12}$ =

7) $\dfrac{10}{12}$ =

8) $\dfrac{3}{4}$ =

9) $\dfrac{1}{5}$ =

10) $\dfrac{5}{20}$ =

Convert the fractions to decimals.

1) $\dfrac{5}{8}$ =

2) $\dfrac{4}{12}$ =

3) $\dfrac{15}{25}$ =

4) $\dfrac{3}{12}$ =

5) $\dfrac{6}{15}$ =

6) $\dfrac{3}{8}$ =

7) $\dfrac{2}{6}$ =

8) $\dfrac{1}{6}$ =

9) $\dfrac{2}{15}$ =

10) $\dfrac{4}{10}$ =

Convert the fractions to decimals.

1) $\dfrac{4}{5}$ =

2) $\dfrac{3}{10}$ =

3) $\dfrac{15}{50}$ =

4) $\dfrac{1}{2}$ =

5) $\dfrac{8}{15}$ =

6) $\dfrac{1}{9}$ =

7) $\dfrac{17}{25}$ =

8) $\dfrac{14}{20}$ =

9) $\dfrac{1}{7}$ =

10) $\dfrac{4}{8}$ =

Convert the fractions to decimals.

1) $\dfrac{3}{5}$ =

2) $\dfrac{9}{15}$ =

3) $\dfrac{7}{10}$ =

4) $\dfrac{8}{12}$ =

5) $\dfrac{8}{10}$ =

6) $\dfrac{8}{30}$ =

7) $\dfrac{2}{20}$ =

8) $\dfrac{4}{6}$ =

9) $\dfrac{18}{25}$ =

10) $\dfrac{19}{20}$ =

Convert the fractions to decimals.

1) $\dfrac{16}{20}$ =

2) $\dfrac{1}{10}$ =

3) $\dfrac{5}{50}$ =

4) $\dfrac{16}{30}$ =

5) $\dfrac{3}{15}$ =

6) $\dfrac{17}{50}$ =

7) $\dfrac{14}{30}$ =

8) $\dfrac{9}{10}$ =

9) $\dfrac{3}{25}$ =

10) $\dfrac{1}{60}$ =

Convert the fractions to decimals.

1) $\dfrac{12}{20}$ =

2) $\dfrac{18}{50}$ =

3) $\dfrac{9}{12}$ =

4) $\dfrac{2}{50}$ =

5) $\dfrac{17}{20}$ =

6) $\dfrac{2}{9}$ =

7) $\dfrac{12}{15}$ =

8) $\dfrac{1}{25}$ =

9) $\dfrac{1}{50}$ =

10) $\dfrac{13}{20}$ =

Convert the fractions to decimals.

1) $\dfrac{17}{20}$ =

2) $\dfrac{21}{25}$ =

3) $\dfrac{30}{40}$ =

4) $\dfrac{11}{15}$ =

5) $\dfrac{19}{25}$ =

6) $\dfrac{17}{30}$ =

7) $\dfrac{3}{40}$ =

8) $\dfrac{16}{40}$ =

9) $\dfrac{23}{40}$ =

10) $\dfrac{8}{25}$ =

Convert the fractions to decimals.

1) $\dfrac{25}{100}$ =

2) $\dfrac{10}{100}$ =

3) $\dfrac{11}{12}$ =

4) $\dfrac{30}{100}$ =

5) $\dfrac{75}{100}$ =

6) $\dfrac{6}{100}$ =

7) $\dfrac{15}{100}$ =

8) $\dfrac{58}{90}$ =

9) $\dfrac{6}{9}$ =

10) $\dfrac{7}{100}$ =

Convert the fractions to decimals.

1) $\dfrac{3}{1000}$ =

2) $\dfrac{8}{90}$ =

3) $\dfrac{60}{100}$ =

4) $\dfrac{2}{100}$ =

5) $\dfrac{80}{150}$ =

6) $\dfrac{14}{200}$ =

7) $\dfrac{20}{100}$ =

8) $\dfrac{25}{90}$ =

9) $\dfrac{25}{1000}$ =

10) $\dfrac{10}{1000}$ =

DECIMALS TO FRACTIONS

Convert the decimals to fractions.

Convert the decimals to fractions.

1) 0.7 =

2) 0.5 =

3) 0.75 =

4) 0.333 =

5) 0.2 =

6) 0.6 =

7) 0.8 =

8) 0.167 =

9) 0.667 =

10) 0.3 =

Convert the decimals to fractions.

1)   0.111   =   6)   0.04   =

2)   0.4   =   7)   0.52   =

3)   0.9   =   8)   0.89   =

4)   0.1   =   9)   0.87   =

5)   0.125   =   10) 0.156 =

Convert the decimals to fractions.

1) 0.28 =

2) 0.58 =

3) 0.13 =

4) 0.06 =

5) 0.28 =

6) 0.325 =

7) 0.31 =

8) 0.71 =

9) 0.17 =

10) 0.53 =

Convert the decimals to fractions.

1) 0.68 =

2) 0.72 =

3) 0.95 =

4) 0.83 =

5) 0.64 =

6) 0.133 =

7) 0.15 =

8) 0.003 =

9) 0.34 =

10) 0.47 =

Convert the decimals to fractions.

1) 0.01 =

2) 0.12 =

3) 0.07 =

4) 0.17 =

5) 0.025 =

6) 0.36 =

7) 0.85 =

8) 0.22 =

9) 0.02 =

10) 0.65 =

Convert the decimals to fractions.

1) 0.84   =

2) 0.73   =

3) 0.76   =

4) 0.567 =

5) 0.075 =

6) 0.08   =

7) 0.575 =

8) 0.32   =

9) 0.05   =

10) 0.03 =

LET'S TRY ANOTHER SET OF ACTIVITIES!

Draw a line to match the fraction to its corresponding decimal form.

Draw a line to match the fraction to its corresponding decimal form.

$\frac{9}{15}$ • • 0.3

$\frac{7}{10}$ • • 0.6

$\frac{3}{10}$ • • 0.27

$\frac{8}{30}$ • • 0.125

$\frac{1}{8}$ • • 0.7

Draw a line to match the fraction to its corresponding decimal form.

$\dfrac{1}{10}$ •	• 0.75
$\dfrac{3}{4}$ •	• 0.95
$\dfrac{18}{25}$ •	• 0.7
$\dfrac{2}{5}$ •	• 0.1
$\dfrac{19}{20}$ •	• 0.72

Draw a line to match the fraction to its corresponding decimal form.

$\dfrac{5}{6}$ •	• 0.13
$\dfrac{58}{90}$ •	• 0.64
$\dfrac{2}{15}$ •	• 0.83
$\dfrac{16}{20}$ •	• 0.1
$\dfrac{5}{50}$ •	• 0.8

Draw a line to match the fraction to its corresponding decimal form.

Fraction		Decimal
$\dfrac{16}{30}$	• •	0.7
$\dfrac{14}{20}$	• •	0.15
$\dfrac{3}{15}$	• •	0.06
$\dfrac{15}{100}$	• •	0.2
$\dfrac{6}{100}$	• •	0.53

Draw a line to match the fraction to its corresponding decimal form.

$\dfrac{8}{10}$ •	• 0.34
$\dfrac{17}{50}$ •	• 0.8
$\dfrac{14}{30}$ •	• 0.07
$\dfrac{9}{10}$ •	• 0.9
$\dfrac{7}{100}$ •	• 0.47

Draw a line to match the fraction to its corresponding decimal form.

$\dfrac{3}{25}$	0.17
$\dfrac{16}{30}$	0.53
$\dfrac{1}{60}$	0.12
$\dfrac{12}{20}$	0.6
$\dfrac{18}{50}$	0.36

Draw a line to match the fraction to its corresponding decimal form.

$\dfrac{2}{50}$	• •	0.09
$\dfrac{2}{9}$	• •	0.85
$\dfrac{17}{20}$	• •	0.6
$\dfrac{60}{100}$	• •	0.22
$\dfrac{8}{90}$	• •	0.04

Draw a line to match the fraction to its corresponding decimal form.

$\dfrac{4}{20}$ •	• 0.6
$\dfrac{5}{20}$ •	• 0.2
$\dfrac{6}{10}$ •	• 0.17
$\dfrac{1}{3}$ •	• 0.33
$\dfrac{1}{6}$ •	• 0.25

Draw a line to match the fraction to its corresponding decimal form.

$\dfrac{3}{10}$ •   • 0.75

$\dfrac{1}{2}$ •   • 0.3

$\dfrac{3}{4}$ •   • 0.53

$\dfrac{8}{15}$ •   • 0.25

$\dfrac{1}{4}$ •   • 0.5

Draw a line to match the fraction to its corresponding decimal form.

$\dfrac{16}{25}$ •	• 0.684
$\dfrac{13}{19}$ •	• 0.27
$\dfrac{9}{15}$ •	• 0.7
$\dfrac{7}{10}$ •	• 0.6
$\dfrac{8}{30}$ •	• 0.64

COMPARISON SYMBOLS

Write the correct Comparison Symbol (>, < or =) in each box.

Write the correct Comparison Symbol (>, < or =) in each box.

1) 3.3 ☐ 0.33

2) 4.96 ☐ 0.496

3) 7.31 ☐ 7.31

4) 6.72 ☐ 6.69

5) 9.06 ☐ 9.01

6) 4.28 ☐ 4.32

7) 5.26 ☐ 5.25

8) 9.05 ☐ 9.1

9) 7.76 ☐ 7.79

10) 2.53 ☐ 0.253

Write the correct Comparison Symbol (>, < or =) in each box.

1) 9.42 ☐ 0.942

2) 8.83 ☐ 8.84

3) 7.11 ☐ 7.18

4) 5.14  0.514

5) 9.35  9.36

6) 0.72 ☐ 0.072

7) 6.21 ☐ 0.621

8) 1.19 ☐ 1.21

9) 9.39 ☐ 9.38

10) 6.83  0.683

Write the correct Comparison Symbol (>, < or =) in each box.

1) $\dfrac{7}{8}$ ☐ $\dfrac{7}{10}$ 6) $\dfrac{1}{10}$ ☐ $\dfrac{2}{3}$

2) $\dfrac{5}{7}$ ☐ $\dfrac{8}{10}$ 7) $\dfrac{3}{9}$ ☐ $\dfrac{1}{4}$

3) $\dfrac{4}{6}$ ☐ $\dfrac{2}{5}$ 8) $\dfrac{3}{5}$ ☐ $\dfrac{1}{2}$

4) $\dfrac{5}{10}$ ☐ $\dfrac{1}{2}$ 9) $\dfrac{1}{2}$ ☐ $\dfrac{2}{8}$

5) $\dfrac{2}{9}$ ☐ $\dfrac{1}{3}$ 10) $\dfrac{9}{10}$ ☐ $\dfrac{3}{7}$

Write the correct Comparison Symbol (>, < or =) in each box.

1) $\dfrac{3}{4}$ ☐ $\dfrac{6}{10}$ 6) $\dfrac{1}{3}$ ☐ $\dfrac{7}{9}$

2) $\dfrac{1}{2}$ ☐ $\dfrac{8}{10}$ 7) $\dfrac{3}{4}$ ☐ $\dfrac{4}{8}$

3) $\dfrac{4}{5}$ ☐ $\dfrac{5}{8}$ 8) $\dfrac{3}{7}$ ☐ $\dfrac{3}{8}$

4) $\dfrac{1}{3}$ ☐ $\dfrac{1}{5}$ 9) $\dfrac{5}{6}$ ☐ $\dfrac{7}{9}$

5) $\dfrac{9}{10}$ ☐ $\dfrac{6}{7}$ 10) $\dfrac{1}{7}$ ☐ $\dfrac{1}{7}$

ANSWERS

FRACTIONS TO DECIMALS

Convert the fractions to decimals.

Convert the fractions to decimals.

1) $\dfrac{1}{12}$ = 0.083

2) $\dfrac{3}{6}$ = 0.5

3) $\dfrac{1}{4}$ = 0.25

4) $\dfrac{6}{8}$ = 0.75

5) $\dfrac{2}{5}$ = 0.4

6) $\dfrac{1}{3}$ = 0.333

7) $\dfrac{2}{3}$ = 0.667

8) $\dfrac{6}{12}$ = 0.5

9) $\dfrac{4}{20}$ = 0.2

10) $\dfrac{2}{4}$ = 0.5

Convert the fractions to decimals.

1) $\dfrac{5}{10}$ = 0.5

2) $\dfrac{2}{8}$ = 0.25

3) $\dfrac{5}{6}$ = 0.833

4) $\dfrac{1}{8}$ = 0.125

5) $\dfrac{6}{10}$ = 0.6

6) $\dfrac{7}{12}$ = 0.583

7) $\dfrac{10}{12}$ = 0.833

8) $\dfrac{3}{4}$ = 0.75

9) $\dfrac{1}{5}$ = 0.2

10) $\dfrac{5}{20}$ = 0.25

Convert the fractions to decimals.

1) $\dfrac{5}{8}$ = 0.625
6) $\dfrac{3}{8}$ = 0.375

2) $\dfrac{4}{12}$ = 0.333
7) $\dfrac{2}{6}$ = 0.333

3) $\dfrac{15}{25}$ = 0.6
8) $\dfrac{1}{6}$ = 0.167

4) $\dfrac{3}{12}$ = 0.25
9) $\dfrac{2}{15}$ = 0.133

5) $\dfrac{6}{15}$ = 0.4
10) $\dfrac{4}{10}$ = 0.4

Convert the fractions to decimals.

1) $\dfrac{4}{5}$ = 0.8
6) $\dfrac{1}{9}$ = 0.111

2) $\dfrac{3}{10}$ = 0.3
7) $\dfrac{17}{25}$ = 0.68

3) $\dfrac{15}{50}$ = 0.3
8) $\dfrac{14}{20}$ = 0.7

4) $\dfrac{1}{2}$ = 0.5
9) $\dfrac{1}{7}$ = 0.143

5) $\dfrac{8}{15}$ = 0.533
10) $\dfrac{4}{8}$ = 0.5

Convert the fractions to decimals.

1) $\frac{3}{5}$ = 0.6

2) $\frac{9}{15}$ = 0.6

3) $\frac{7}{10}$ = 0.7

4) $\frac{8}{12}$ = 0.667

5) $\frac{8}{10}$ = 0.8

6) $\frac{8}{30}$ = 0.27

7) $\frac{2}{20}$ = 0.1

8) $\frac{4}{6}$ = 0.667

9) $\frac{18}{25}$ = 0.72

10) $\frac{19}{20}$ = 0.95

Convert the fractions to decimals.

1) $\frac{16}{20}$ = 0.8

2) $\frac{1}{10}$ = 0.1

3) $\frac{5}{50}$ = 0.1

4) $\frac{16}{30}$ = 0.533

5) $\frac{3}{15}$ = 0.2

6) $\frac{17}{50}$ = 0.34

7) $\frac{14}{30}$ = 0.47

8) $\frac{9}{10}$ = 0.9

9) $\frac{3}{25}$ = 0.12

10) $\frac{1}{60}$ = 0.17

Convert the fractions to decimals.

1) $\dfrac{12}{20}$ = 0.6

2) $\dfrac{18}{50}$ = 0.36

3) $\dfrac{9}{12}$ = 0.75

4) $\dfrac{2}{50}$ = 0.04

5) $\dfrac{17}{20}$ = 0.85

6) $\dfrac{2}{9}$ = 0.22

7) $\dfrac{12}{15}$ = 0.8

8) $\dfrac{1}{25}$ = 0.04

9) $\dfrac{1}{50}$ = 0.02

10) $\dfrac{13}{20}$ = 0.65

Convert the fractions to decimals.

1) $\dfrac{17}{20}$ = 0.85

2) $\dfrac{21}{25}$ = 0.84

3) $\dfrac{30}{40}$ = 0.75

4) $\dfrac{11}{15}$ = 0.73

5) $\dfrac{19}{25}$ = 0.76

6) $\dfrac{17}{30}$ = 0.57

7) $\dfrac{3}{40}$ = 0.075

8) $\dfrac{16}{40}$ = 0.4

9) $\dfrac{23}{40}$ = 0.575

10) $\dfrac{8}{25}$ = 0.32

ACTIVITY NO:  9

Convert the fractions to decimals.

1) $\frac{25}{100}$ = 0.25

2) $\frac{10}{100}$ = 0.1

3) $\frac{11}{12}$ = 0.917

4) $\frac{30}{100}$ = 0.3

5) $\frac{75}{100}$ = 0.75

6) $\frac{6}{100}$ = 0.06

7) $\frac{15}{100}$ = 0.15

8) $\frac{58}{90}$ = 0.64

9) $\frac{6}{9}$ = 0.667

10) $\frac{7}{100}$ = 0.07

FRACTIONS TO DECIMALS **ACTIVITY NO:** 10

Convert the fractions to decimals.

1) $\frac{3}{1000}$ = 0.003

2) $\frac{8}{90}$ = 0.09

3) $\frac{60}{100}$ = 0.6

4) $\frac{2}{100}$ = 0.02

5) $\frac{80}{150}$ = 0.53

6) $\frac{14}{200}$ = 0.07

7) $\frac{20}{100}$ = 0.2

8) $\frac{25}{90}$ = 0.28

9) $\frac{25}{1000}$ = 0.025

10) $\frac{10}{1000}$ = 0.01

DECIMALS TO FRACTIONS

Convert the decimals to fractions.

Convert the decimals to fractions.

1) $0.7 = \dfrac{7}{10}$

2) $0.5 = \dfrac{1}{2}$

3) $0.75 = \dfrac{3}{4}$

4) $0.333 = \dfrac{1}{3}$

5) $0.2 = \dfrac{1}{5}$

6) $0.6 = \dfrac{3}{5}$

7) $0.8 = \dfrac{4}{5}$

8) $0.167 = \dfrac{1}{6}$

9) $0.667 = \dfrac{2}{3}$

10) $0.3 = \dfrac{3}{10}$

Convert the decimals to fractions.

1) $0.111 = \dfrac{1}{9}$

2) $0.4 = \dfrac{2}{5}$

3) $0.9 = \dfrac{9}{10}$

4) $0.1 = \dfrac{1}{10}$

5) $0.125 = \dfrac{1}{8}$

6) $0.04 = \dfrac{1}{25}$

7) $0.52 = \dfrac{13}{25}$

8) $0.89 = \dfrac{8}{9}$

9) $0.87 = \dfrac{13}{15}$

10) $0.156 = \dfrac{7}{45}$

Convert the decimals to fractions.

1) $0.28 = \dfrac{5}{18}$

2) $0.58 = \dfrac{7}{12}$

3) $0.13 = \dfrac{13}{100}$

4) $0.06 = \dfrac{3}{50}$

5) $0.28 = \dfrac{7}{28}$

6) $0.325 = \dfrac{13}{40}$

7) $0.31 = \dfrac{14}{45}$

8) $0.71 = \dfrac{5}{7}$

9) $0.17 = \dfrac{1}{6}$

10) $0.53 = \dfrac{8}{15}$

Convert the decimals to fractions.

1) $0.68 = \dfrac{17}{25}$

2) $0.72 = \dfrac{18}{25}$

3) $0.95 = \dfrac{19}{20}$

4) $0.83 = \dfrac{5}{6}$

5) $0.64 = \dfrac{29}{45}$

6) $0.133 = \dfrac{2}{15}$

7) $0.15 = \dfrac{3}{20}$

8) $0.003 = \dfrac{3}{1000}$

9) $0.34 = \dfrac{17}{50}$

10) $0.47 = \dfrac{7}{15}$

Convert the decimals to fractions.

1) $0.01 = \dfrac{1}{100}$

2) $0.12 = \dfrac{3}{25}$

3) $0.07 = \dfrac{7}{100}$

4) $0.17 = \dfrac{1}{60}$

5) $0.025 = \dfrac{1}{40}$

6) $0.36 = \dfrac{9}{25}$

7) $0.85 = \dfrac{17}{20}$

8) $0.22 = \dfrac{2}{9}$

9) $0.02 = \dfrac{1}{50}$

10) $0.65 = \dfrac{13}{20}$

Convert the decimals to fractions.

1) $0.84 = \dfrac{21}{25}$

2) $0.73 = \dfrac{11}{15}$

3) $0.76 = \dfrac{19}{25}$

4) $0.567 = \dfrac{17}{30}$

5) $0.075 = \dfrac{3}{40}$

6) $0.08 = \dfrac{1}{12}$

7) $0.575 = \dfrac{23}{40}$

8) $0.32 = \dfrac{8}{25}$

9) $0.05 = \dfrac{1}{20}$

10) $0.03 = \dfrac{3}{100}$

Draw a line to match the fraction
to its corresponding decimal form.

Draw a line to match the fraction to its corresponding decimal form.

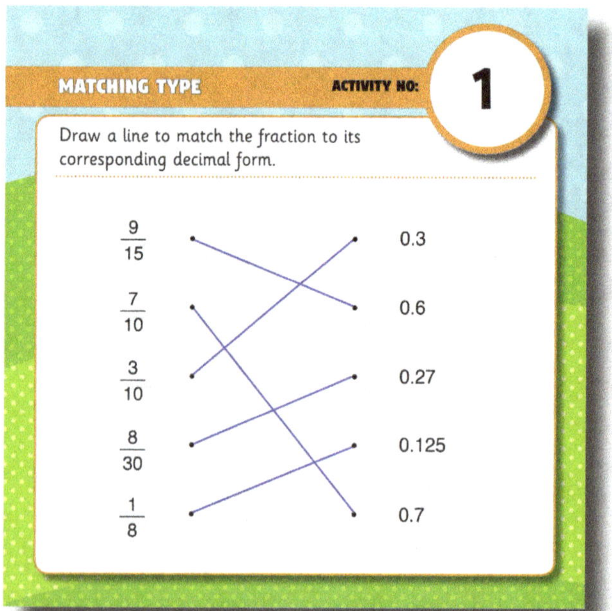

Draw a line to match the fraction to its corresponding decimal form.

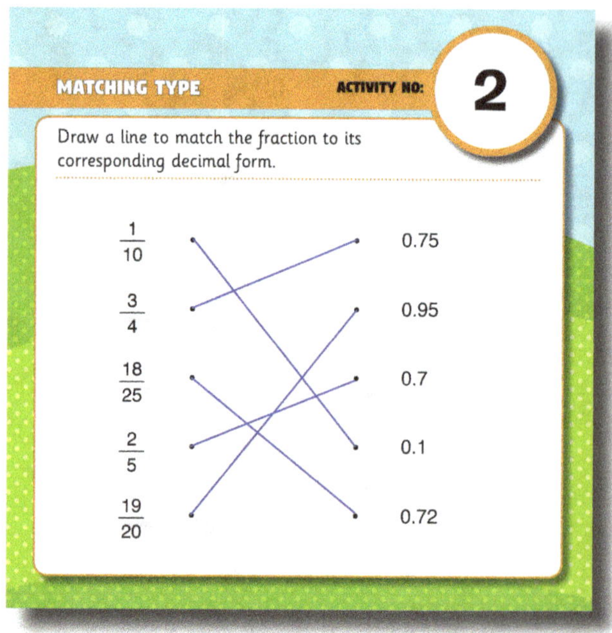

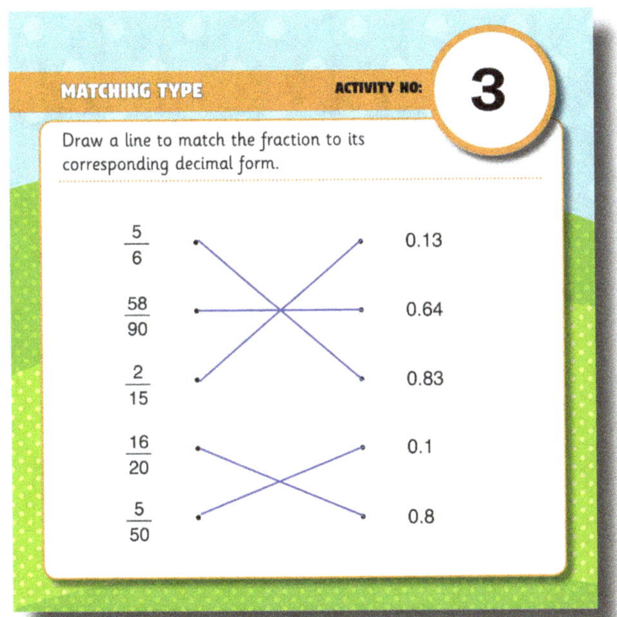

MATCHING TYPE
ACTIVITY NO: 3
Draw a line to match the fraction to its corresponding decimal form.
5/6
58/90
2/15
16/20
5/50
0.13
0.64
0.83
0.1
0.8

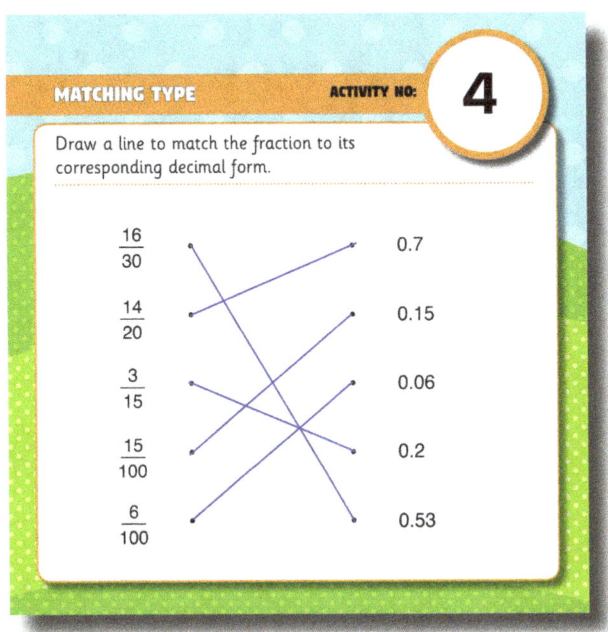

MATCHING TYPE
ACTIVITY NO: 4
Draw a line to match the fraction to its corresponding decimal form.
16/30
14/20
3/15
15/100
6/100
0.7
0.15
0.06
0.2
0.53

ACTIVITY NO: **5**

Draw a line to match the fraction to its corresponding decimal form.

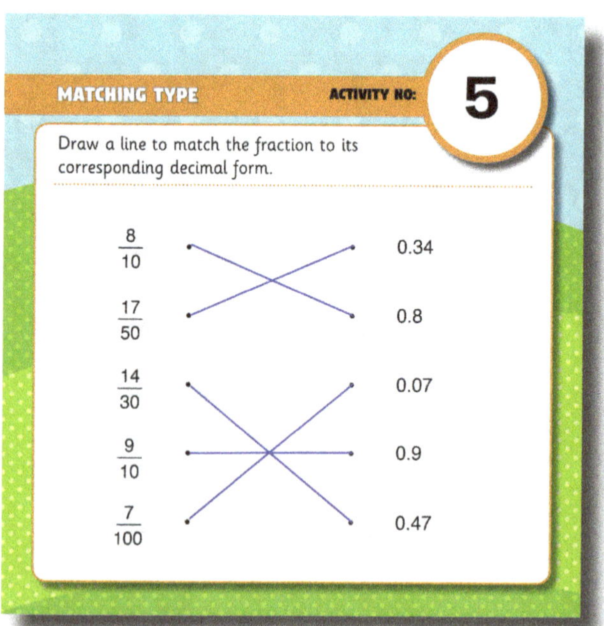

ACTIVITY NO: **6**

Draw a line to match the fraction to its corresponding decimal form.

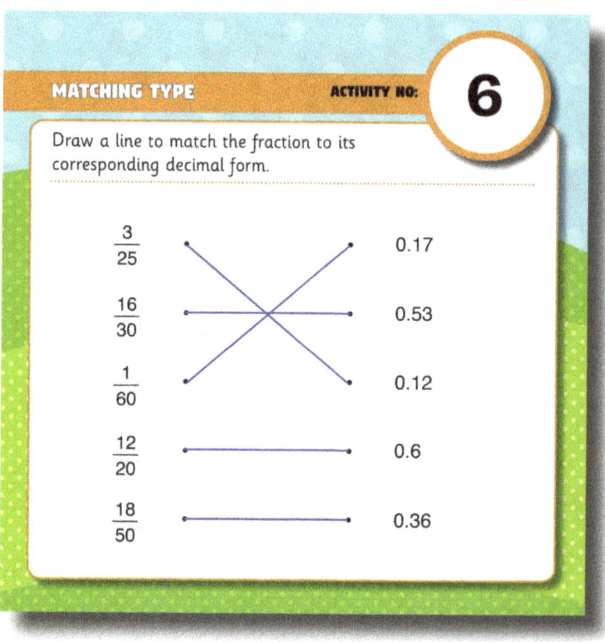

Draw a line to match the fraction to its corresponding decimal form.

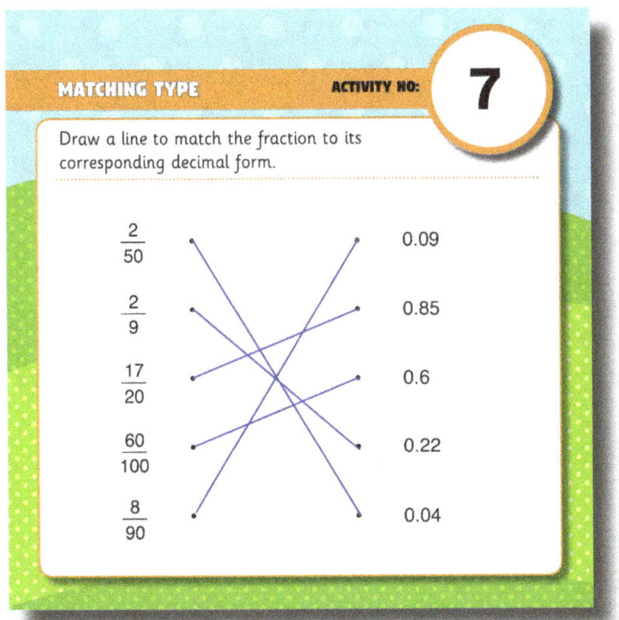

Draw a line to match the fraction to its corresponding decimal form.

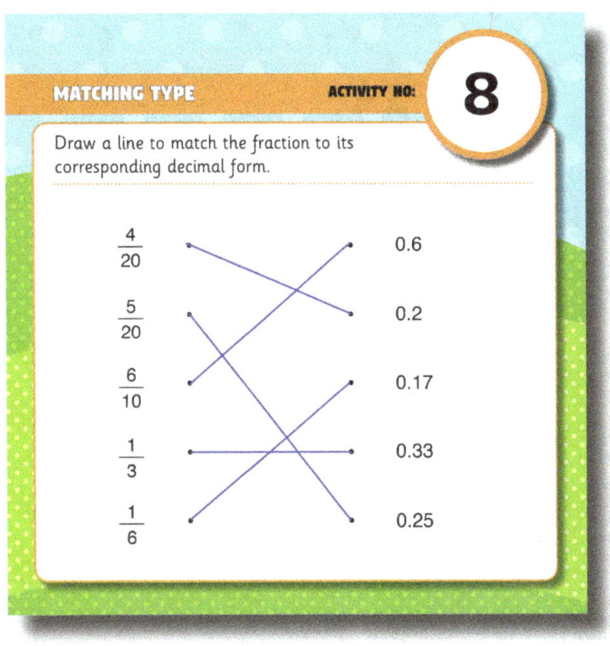

Draw a line to match the fraction to its corresponding decimal form.

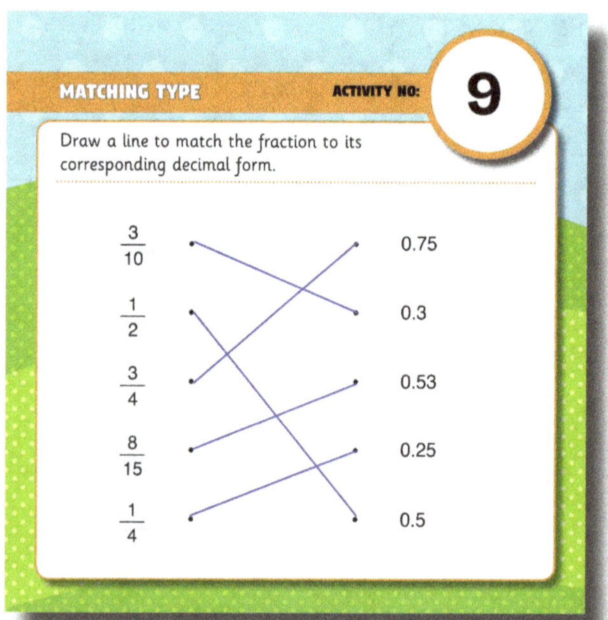

Draw a line to match the fraction to its corresponding decimal form.

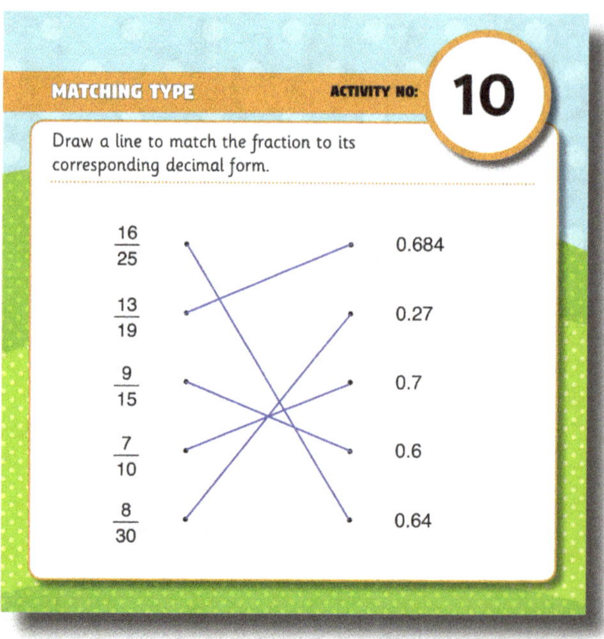

COMPARISON SYMBOLS

Write the correct Comparison Symbol (>, < or =) in each box.

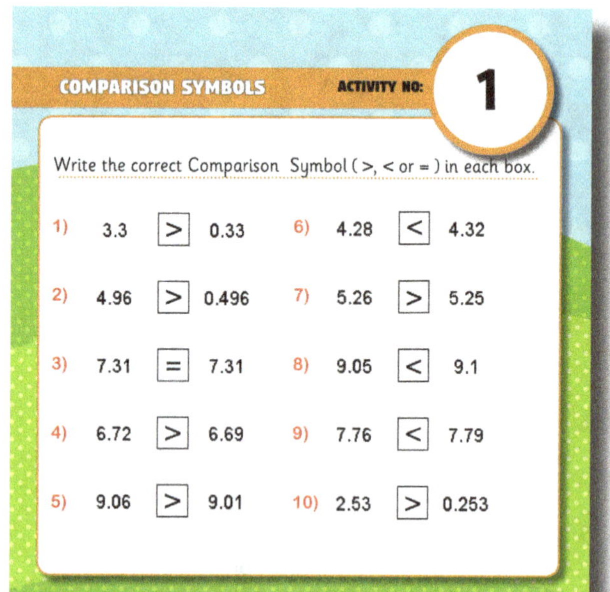

COMPARISON SYMBOLS
ACTIVITY NO: 1

Write the correct Comparison Symbol (>, < or =) in each box.

1) 3.3 > 0.33
2) 4.96 > 0.496
3) 7.31 = 7.31
4) 6.72 > 6.69
5) 9.06 > 9.01
6) 4.28 < 4.32
7) 5.26 > 5.25
8) 9.05 < 9.1
9) 7.76 < 7.79
10) 2.53 > 0.253

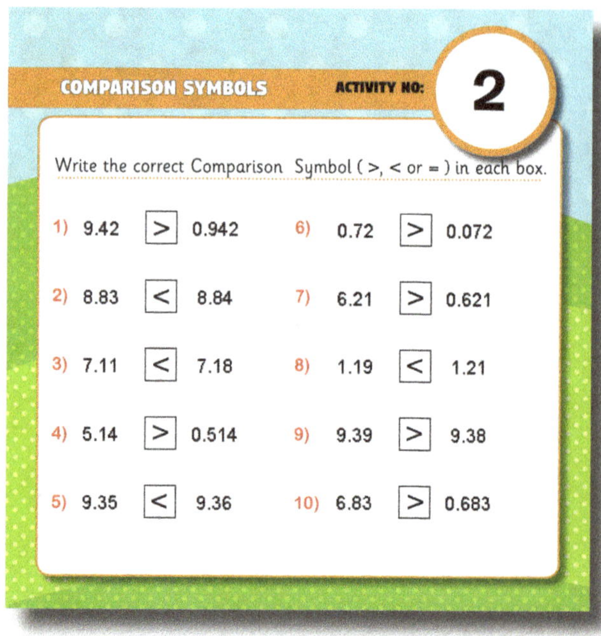

COMPARISON SYMBOLS
ACTIVITY NO: 2

Write the correct Comparison Symbol (>, < or =) in each box.

1) 9.42 > 0.942
2) 8.83 < 8.84
3) 7.11 < 7.18
4) 5.14 > 0.514
5) 9.35 < 9.36
6) 0.72 > 0.072
7) 6.21 > 0.621
8) 1.19 < 1.21
9) 9.39 > 9.38
10) 6.83 > 0.683

Write the correct Comparison Symbol (>, < or =) in each box.

#	Left	Symbol	Right	#	Left	Symbol	Right
1)	$\frac{7}{8}$	>	$\frac{7}{10}$	6)	$\frac{1}{10}$	<	$\frac{2}{3}$
2)	$\frac{5}{7}$	<	$\frac{8}{10}$	7)	$\frac{3}{9}$	>	$\frac{1}{4}$
3)	$\frac{4}{6}$	>	$\frac{2}{5}$	8)	$\frac{3}{5}$	>	$\frac{1}{2}$
4)	$\frac{5}{10}$	=	$\frac{1}{2}$	9)	$\frac{1}{2}$	>	$\frac{2}{8}$
5)	$\frac{2}{9}$	<	$\frac{1}{3}$	10)	$\frac{9}{10}$	>	$\frac{3}{7}$

Write the correct Comparison Symbol (>, < or =) in each box.

#	Left	Symbol	Right	#	Left	Symbol	Right
1)	$\frac{3}{4}$	>	$\frac{6}{10}$	6)	$\frac{1}{3}$	<	$\frac{7}{9}$
2)	$\frac{1}{2}$	<	$\frac{8}{10}$	7)	$\frac{3}{4}$	>	$\frac{4}{8}$
3)	$\frac{4}{5}$	>	$\frac{5}{8}$	8)	$\frac{3}{7}$	>	$\frac{3}{8}$
4)	$\frac{1}{3}$	>	$\frac{1}{5}$	9)	$\frac{5}{6}$	>	$\frac{7}{9}$
5)	$\frac{9}{10}$	>	$\frac{6}{7}$	10)	$\frac{1}{7}$	=	$\frac{1}{7}$

Visit
BABY PROFESSOR
EDUCATION KIDS
www.BabyProfessorBooks.com
to download Free Baby Professor eBooks
and view our catalog of new and exciting
Children's Books